HE

MUST

END

HE MUST END

poetry and prose

VHON MICHAEL

HE MUST END

For Xaniel,

Xaniel,
I gazed upon galaxies when I met you.

There are things I regret
There are some I wish to take back
There are moments I look back to
And seconds spent wishing I can come back

There are times when I am miles away
I wonder off to the wonderland where you're at
To wish to be there, to wish I stop
To wish I could close my eyes, pass that

Just to be clear
I do feel rage, I do feel hate
But I hate my mistake
Not you

WHEN DAYS BECOME BLURRY

I hate getting angry
because then I'd have to
tell myself lies
not to believe
what my mind tells me
that I'm the mirror of my father
   a spitting image
      a doppelgänger
         a shadow buried deeply into the woods

a wild boar
lashing on things
without second thoughts
   minutes long
      hours repentance to forget
         what the days made me remember
           what months of depression couldn't take
              what years couldn't bury

what

    a

        lifetime

            couldn't

                erase

I hate to be angry at myself
because then I'd run out
of lies to lullaby myself with
to ease the pain of knowing
there is a chance—
I could become like my father.

ODE TO THE OLD POETS

I used to be hypocrite
Mimicking what my elders did
They wrote so much
About their families
And how they've been loved well
It made me faint

I wrote then so much
About how my parents loved me well
How my family accepted me
Like a letter of request, open letter
Of what I require
To be able to write well
About my personal experiences,
Stories I can sell
To air my grievances.

Did it hurt?
Was the idea of leaving me painful to you too?
Did it hurt having to decide whether to stay or not?
Was it maiming having to think about the memories?
Nostalgic and tragic, our warmth tale had to end painfully.

Did it hurt?
Was the thought of me brought you tears?
Did it sting when I constantly cross your mind?
Does my name still leave a bitter-sweet taste in your tongue?
Dreaming it slow and tender—you still ended it swiftly.

Did it heal you?
Was leaving me really that good for you?
Did it still ache when you unconsciously call for my name?
Was it restoring, when you left what was haven?
You longed for something new and exciting, dared
and still daring.

Was it you or was it really me?
Was it the dream of something new or the nightmare of the past?
Was it yearning or was it the horror brought by your illicit acts?
Do you still talk to the constellations about me like you used to?

I do still write tales about you for the stars to read
But just staring at the night sky for so long
Long enough just watching at them starts to make sense
They start writing stories about the world
Like visions envisioned from the past to the future
Folk tales of broken records and dead dreams
I still whisper your name in the air like a wish
I do when a shooting star flashes before my eyes
Like a goddamn dandelion floating in the air
You poisoned the only air I could breathe
The moon still tells me stories about you
Even though I'm fucking tired, but I still sit
And stare and listen to every wrenching words
You're no longer my world just my memories of you

Today, I was called pretty
Kind words enveloped my cheeks
Kinder embraces wrapping
Kindest gestures sealed with love

Oh, to be called sweet
Angels risen and singing above
To be held in an embrace
Be trapped in his dashing gaze

He called me precious
Priceless being traded everything
His love a room so spacious
His pieces a memory ink tattooed in my being

Oh, to be loved so dearly
You can feel him even in absence
Oh, to have someone who is surely
For me, he called me pretty.

Soft were your strokes of the brush
Feeling of unknown lines behind my back
I painted you with colors, you painted me gold
Made a canvas out of myself for you
I've asked you to draw something true

All my nightmares, all your daydreams
All these feelings painted golden
You covered my naked body in paint,
I was your demon and you were my saint
I worship your body and I'm so insane

You've finished the art;
Now it's time for us to set apart

the unasked

but how can I say *goodbye*
when all I wanted to say was *hello*
and *please don't let me go.*

THE THIEF

I look into his deep enticing eyes
Full of longing. Heart breaking.
A jar of twinkling stars and
Feelings felt along with the night sky.

His elegies sang like a ballad.
A melody of hurt and knowing.
A trip back to before,
All mourning, darkness growing.

A replay of the greatest piece ever written.
All those moments I'd say
I love you against his lips.
Never knowing the prices I'd have to pay.

It breaks me to see you fall apart
And it breaks me even more
To see the world we have built
For us both falling apart.

Just like Clyde losing Bonnie.
I never imagined for this day to come.
How I wore my heart on my sleeve—
And you took it like a thief.

foolish

two boys kissing
jaws clenching
hearts warming
but love is fleeting

for Xaniel,

does it surprise You I was never my own homebody?
I spent years renting in people's love to shelter my yearning
lit up stoves cooking down medium all my untold feelings
Your tenderness a greenhouse screening my verdure passion
a lighthouse to my port guiding all my wandering pieces
I was showered with all Your ocean deep affection
until I was drowning and made a home out of You
I was lost at first but it was clear midway
home was never really a place,
You made me realize that.

I never appreciated the beauty of *hello*s and *goodbye*s when I first met you. But at this very moment, it's hard to say *goodbye* when I know that tomorrow I won't be getting a *hello*.

DEAD AIR

It's better letting go sometimes, isn't it?
No longer letting the rope injure our palms
Fortune telling no longer sparks nostalgia
Yearning for tomorrow as if it was yesterday
No longer letting some pause damage our work
And some dead air cause confusions
Communication was never really the key
We're playing games no longer hail a victor
As if contending with a giant using a double-edge sword
Performing with masks and covers in a ballroom
Not letting our bare naked fleshes grind against
All the fleshes and bones in this lore
No longer letting some dead air suffocate us
And bring some mystery into our tale
We try our best to fill every second with epic scales

Sometimes I think about killing myself;
Where satisfaction meets guilt,
Laid bare on the evergreen undying;
When love and lost become stilt.

I imagine myself flying at times,
Freely hovering over missed times.
When paranoia creeps to collect debts,
Payments to feelings I owed no one.

All these familiar oafs make me think:
Life seems bearable in present times,
Past midnight when darkness broke out
All my promises tilled in times of drought.

I am a devout to faceless figurines.
About balance when living is without;
Throughout I paint my sinless skins,
Through thins I give out verdure sprouts.

Sometimes I cut myself with knife:
Seemingly gentle to innocent life.
I hold my passions so dearly like nets
Of safety of freedom, of freedom from bets.

I say 'thank you' to the stars
And to the sound of silence:
Creeping me up with peace and bliss.

I say 'thank you' to the dawn,
The peaceful silence before sunset,
And two twinkling sparks my eyes meet.

I say 'thank you' to the rays of the sun,
And the unusually comforting smell
Before thousands of droplets fall from the sky.

My life has always been in backwards and reversed:
I meet darkness with delight, never hoping
Of peace in these disastrous daylights.

U DESERVE

I am so tired of being a dandelion
Blown by the winds of uncertainty
of love you thought is written in the belts of Orion
of love actually written as a tragedy.

Oh, to be called pretty.
Even when he realizes you're not;
To be played by love so witty,
In a hurricane I am caught.

Take me with you when you go.
I am not kinder than you deserve.
You are worthy of love that show—
Oh, to be with you even as a reserve.

"You are kinder than I deserve",
Your words cut through sharper than a knife
Segued with kinder words to preserve,
I am a dandelion blown, gone in a blink of light.

Loving you comes in waves
And each day as I woke
I keep sinking deeper and deeper—
Dragged to the bottom of the ocean
Resurfacing every now and then
Watch you walk on the shore
Collecting shells, star gazing
Watch you walk on the shores
As waves hit your leg
It's you, I keep missing.

And if
Loving you comes in tidal waves,
Tonight, I am drowning.

Oh, to be loved and not get lost
Be cherished with sufficient affection
To write him poetry to last
Be appreciated without being in the selection

I am the sidelines
Stationed posts in the outskirts
Of grayish scales and weights
This time to love without hurt

To be loved and never get lost
Not tethered but freely trapped
To be seen and be protected
Not taken for granted or wasted

Oh, to be loved and be secured
Held tightly with passion and wanting
Oh, to be held forever with care
Gentle embraces in the morning rare

Keep wanting
Keep needing
Keep falling in love
Over and over

I'm not fond of saying 'good bye'
and so, I say "hi"—
when I meet, I beg people
again, and again
"care to stop by, and maybe
just maybe play with my petty little heart
and then ruin my life?" or
so I say, *"Would you mind*
staying for a while, try
to know each other and
maybe develop feelings—
and then leave forever?"
and then we try
not to see each other…

Just come back right in
when I get ahold of things
try to play with my hands
take then everything away
and say your "see you sooner",
and all my mishaps, your mayhem
and those nights I'd always try.

SECOND

I wish to be met with the same energy
of same excitement and glee
To be held gently with passion
of the same love and affection

When you said you liked her
Did you mean like a dear friend
or like she makes your breathe hitch
and give you butterflies in your stomach

Was I fulfilling as her
Was she winning in all parts
Was she the person of your dreams
Something I couldn't become

You met me halfway heartbreak
In the halls of her between me
To choose between us both
is already heartbreaking for me

I've counted all the tiles in the bathroom
From the days I've been without you
All those nights thinking
"When will I ever hear you again sing?"

All those troubles and bubbles,
Sweetcakes and milkshakes,
And all the kisses we have shared,
Hidden in the great lakes.

All my '*what if*'s
And your '*could have been*'s
All the doubts we've shared
And regrets in the eyes seen.

All your daylights
And my northern lights
And the nights we've used to fight—
Until you're no longer in my sight.

It hurts to keep writing your name
But I can't stop myself
It hurts to say it
But I can't let you go

I look for you in the sci-fi aisle
Whenever I visit bookstores
Hoping to find you there
Immersed in your favorite lore

I draw your face in my mind
Keep your palette memorized
I read your TO BE READ list for you
I stay up at night finishing
All our impending list of series
For us, alone I watched.

THE RELIGION

I never really believe in God
Not sure if I trust fate and destiny
I met you in pure uncertainty
My uber getting late is the one to thank
There are no outside forces playing here
I don't believe in folklores and forever
No trust in the name of unconditional love
Confused whether it's planned or you're authentic
No backup plans and ulterior motives
Your eyes they scare me to death,
I pray you stay longer than planned
Get on my knees and hail your measured love
I commit all my devotion in you
And worship with every single piece of me
My yearning you disprove
My lust you consume
My desire you intensify
I commune every night before my head hits the pillow
Cry that each day as I woke yours is next to mine

the flight

You used to tell me how
your day went. Your crazy,

stories and finds during
your walks: flowers, the sky,

our love dissipating. I asked
how you are and you told me

you were leaving. Never once
ever answered my "how are you?"

left opened. Not once since then
you ever came back since

you found home in someone else.

WANTING

I hate that I still long for your touch / trace
your smile with the stars / how I see your face
wherever I go / and how I have been / wanting /
to answer all your voice messages

I hate that I can't delete your voice mail /
or delete every single memory of you / how
your lips are touching mine / while you are
hugging me to keep me intact / until / you
decided / to let me break apart

I hate how I still whisper your name / and
dream of wanting you back again / but
the memories of you / saying we
should stop / stopped me / from running
back to your arms again.

they say moments last forever—
but do I want it?

I don't like breaking;
going back to places
realizing
memories were made
but can only ever go back
to the places
but never to those moments.

SPILLED INKS

Why is it that every time I start to write a poem / by starting with 'you' / I always end up writing bad things about you / as if there were no good things / that I felt / even though most of them were actually good / why is it that I always paint you black?

As if you were a stain resistant to my bleach / as if you were supposed to be dark / even if you weren't / maybe because when you accidentally painted me black / you tainted the words I could use to describe every single part of you.

p.s.

if you don't know how to
keep someone anymore,
please tell them.
if you do, do so gently,
it might hurt a little
it might hurt so much
but it will pass.
completely disappearing
like a phantom
destroys.

never become the
monster
you've been hating
your whole life.

I knew you were trouble (*after Taylor Swift's song*)

But I still jumped right into you / like you were just 20 feet cliff / towards the open ocean / of freedom / an open space where I thought I'd feel I belong / like wide open arms waiting for me to embrace fully.

I still danced with you / even if you were the heartache / that feeling when the flower died / all my sadness turned into tears / but I will still walk with you / even if I was breaking.

Is it normal to hurt a little
when you look at him?

TOOK ADVANTAGE

for Llorenç,

it was so nice knowing you
and how you welcomed me
with warm hugs and smiles

it was so nice to have a friend
with whom you can tell all your
never-been-shared stories
you've kept in your jar all these years

tell me where we both went wrong
and how we're lost in translation
I know it's not because you're Spanish
and I'm Filipino, it's unsettling

or was it because I come to you
to tell you about this boy
and how he was my *what if*s
only to find out it was you all along

I am so sorry that I lied
About who I really like
I was confused and didn't know
If it was you or my idea of you

INDIGO SKIES

Remember when we used to
Eat at this certain café
Near the port to uncertainty
Enjoying the beauty of the sky

How sweet that you remember
My usual order, our usual spot
Our usual time to watch the indigo skies,

Now here I am back at this café
Waiting for my ship to sail
In this port of heartbreak getaway
I don't know if I should still stay

Do you remember
My usual order, our usual spot
It's now where I'm breaking

To tell you a secret
I still remember your usual order
I still see your face in my head
How you'd smile as the sun sets
We wave good bye to sailing ships

REMINDER

I almost threw the notebook where
I write all my poetry and uncertainty
Not wanting to get reminded of you
But then I remember most times I miss you,

I'd lose the only reminder
That you forgot, and I am
The only one left remembering

INHERITANCE

I've been told
good people let things pass
I've been taught
to shut up
        when adults tell me my future
        recite my weaknesses and failures
        tell me I'm never good enough
to look down
        in shame when they shame me
        break down when they break me
to never
        talk back because good people
        never talks back
        they never defend themselves
to break in silence
to fail in silence
to cry in silence
        because you can never be proud
        of things like these
only successes should be paraded
only my failures should be paraded
        when it's to their advantage
but I should keep quiet
never talk
never write this.

THE SUN RAY

I wish that every sun ray that touches my skin
Cleanses me and cleanses every bit of you
That covers me, all those bits and pieces of you
That lingers, how your name still covering my lips,
How those sparkles now illuminating my eyes—
How I wish that with every sun ray that touches
Me, I forget a piece of you that haunts me.

OUT OF THE WOODS

Hush boy
breaking is now an option
you're free to wipe your tears
without the background noises
telling you only weak people cry
without the eyes of the people
whose hobby is to talk about
other people's lives
like a sport
You're free now
wandering in a new place

breathing
breaking
but finally smiling
liberated from the wild
that preys.

THE DREAMERS

'*Estoy llorando ahora mismo*' I told you
You tell me to close my eyes and try to calm
'*No se como calmarme*' I speak to you
And you replied back in Español, '*lo siento*'

Imagine if we were the dreams
We've told each other before
Secrets we're comfortable spitting
Songs sang and we're singing

Your whimsical satires
My smart comebacks
Exchanges of silent breaths
And morning whimpers

I tell you my demons
You draw me wings
Oh how sweet to tell you my dreams
Even the failed ones I'm still singing

We've always been the dreamers
Society of dead poets and broken poems
I dream of you every time my head hits the pillow
Dreaming of you being next to me soon

JOURNAL

tomorrow is not ours
to see, so you see
we only have today
to make history
but we should never
keep looking back
home isn't in the past
it's here now,
make today count

ENIGMA

Was being puzzling gave you satisfaction?
Validation you've been longing for your whole life
Was it completing that you were consuming everybody else?
Ruining buildings that are close to being finished
Was being satisfied gave you power?
All your built-up sadness trashed on others
Was ruining other people gave you madness?
Is it why you chose me? 'cause you know I'd always press
The self-destruct button every time you ask me to

SENTINELS

I've been taught
to never question
only rebels do that

but as I grew older
I've noticed
Only intellects do that

the rest have been tethered
the rest have been blinded
the rest have been scared

some were left behind
some were silenced

writing this
I'm raising the flag
for those who will come
after me
passing down the torch
that have been passed to me
by those who came before me

the silent were safe
because they were loud enough

I'm sounding the alarm.

VANDAL

Did you blink?
When I was being choked to death at the edge of the world
Were you there when I had needed a hand to hold
Was it you that push me towards the death I now hold

Did you blink?
That I still sing your name like a ballad I bled
On pieces of crumpled paper that cut my skin
That gave me nightmares in the name of forgetting you

Did you blink?
Was cutting me off your only choice to survive
Was it a matter of life and death for you to do it
Was it all that mattered to you at the moment

Would you open your eyes?
When you're not only saying your goodbyes
Or moments when you have to hold my hand forever
Not only when you have to give my hand to others

I didn't ask to be trained
to be taught how to be
strong or brave
I needed to be safe
I needed to be loved

And then they tell me
I didn't speak up
I tried but I've been silenced
I've never been voiceless,
*If only they could hear
my faint whispers*

TETHER

In dreams I cry his name,
of charlatan and fever dreams,
I scream everything in his wonderland.
All those longing tethered madness.

I paint myself with dark colors.
In stillness I find peace.
His name goes crazy overtime,
carrying me towards the end time.

WORLD WAR X

How hard is it for us
to say we're sorry?
We could have used the time
we spent in more arguing

in more resentment
in more fighting
in more silent treatments
in more breaking

to aiding the broken
to building ourselves back up
to ending this war

If only we were brave enough
to say we were sorry

THE BIG BANG THEORY

I told you physics is the love of my life
Been obsessed with it since I was four years old
Theorizing has always been my thing
Collecting all *what if* and *could have been* like shells

Bang. The sound of the beginning of everything
Of what we know to be *our* universe
A paradise of common and unusual
Of what we thought to be the very best

Bang. A fascinating light illuminated our world
I held your hand thinking it's the last time
I pulled you close to my very heart
I told you the secrets I've never told anyone before

Bang. It wasn't the universe reforming
What I thought to be a beginning of the most fascinating thing
Was the sound of silence creeping in
Sound of the self-destruct button you slip in my pocket

Bang. The sound of the start of our ending
As you head towards someone else
A promise of a paradise is what you'll be selling
You're not only a charlatan but also a man expert in stealing

HURRY UP, KIDS

Painting our faces red
Practicing our lines
Reminding where we should be
A dry-run of this reality

The show is about to start

IMPOSSIBLE EXPANSE

I no longer am scared of staying adrift
Such thing does no longer mean not existing
Nor only existing merely in between
No loss shall no longer be gained
We need not to sacrifice what we love
In the name of keeping the gap small
It will always grow and grow wider
But such expanse means bigger room
Wider space for such wider volume
Of all the feelings we could ever muster
No longer does possible looking alike impossible
We say, "such things merely exist in nightmares"
And in dreams we grow immense
What we are and all the things that makes us
Stretches to something that illuminates
Even the darkest of this glum world

MIGRATORY BIRDS, TOO, I GUESS

and if we were losers
we find ourselves cuddled up
in some random places:

maybe a bar
maybe a park
maybe a museum
maybe even a church

to let ourselves be free
from these troubling situations

There's nothing more that I love
Better than being lost in his azure eyes
Dazed in unconsciousness and innocence
Glory there might be, of something else
Be held captive in those glimmers
Those that contest all the shades of blue
There's nothing more better than *him* hue.

PENSIVE

maybe we hold the power
over our hearts and minds
we just force ourselves to think
we've given up power to others
only to give up responsibility
and being held accountable
maybe it hurts a little bit too

His voice a dulcet gift from the skies
Seeping wanderlust through mellow sounds
His desire my melodramatic suspense
Weeping and longing for an escape route
His tunes dance around the haven
Melodies run through the gaps between his teeth
His icy utterance drowns my melancholy
Not anymore, a dispirited phantom in his ardor

ENDED CALL

How many times do you have to scream at me like I was dumb enough to not understand every single word that comes out of your mouth? How many times do you have to hit my face for you to realize that I can get things right?

Every call that you make with me, all I ever hear are the screams of madness coming from your end of the line every time I stutter because of the fear that I might say the wrong words and you might end the call.

Every time I answer, every time you hang up, every ended call wakes me up. The moment you spoke the words confessing your hate for me, the thing I did really save my life. Okay.

You kept me as a memento locked away in time
My crestfallen heart, your piercing crypts
Paraded me as a deranged paramour from before
Delirious *bitch* marked of pieces of lovers before
My lucid dreams, your incredulous thinking
Tearing through the crowd of silence and despair
I write this book as a memoir of how *you* died
Right before you even fade away, I did it
Wholeheartedly, I did it completely.

flashes

capture you and me
in every angle free
this art of photography
you and me, a memory

We could have had all the universe
Yet we turned our backs on it as if we didn't dream of it
You pushed me to the edge when things were breaking
I expected you to be the one to make things easy for me

We could have had it all
Yet you chose to turn us back around because you were scared
You dragged me to the bottom of the ocean
And you expected me not to see all those

HOLOGRAMS

you had this image of him
projected inside of your head
at the crossroads of what
he is and should be

you cling onto this idea
fixated character who doesn't exist
dwelled much, romanticized what
he is and should be

you had these holograms
of the perfect prince charming
but you have to choose, what
he is or should be

How many pits do I *need* to fall into
before finding the right path?

WE ARE A TREE SCORCHED IN FLAMES
AFTER A THUNDER STRUCK

in your bed we lay heated
flashed and panting naked
I pointed to your bedside table
filled with books you recently read
I pointed to the other direction
a wall filled with CDs and vinyl
you tell me all about Earth
and how heaven is a myth
and hell isn't

you tell me I should stop
with all my witchcraft bullshit
told me how nature can be felt
just by grounding ourselves
you're scared that if I slip
I'll burn in hell

Honey,
hell is here
our house is on fire
our Earth is up in flames
we lay heated in your bed
panting after a good night sex.

you burn my skin with your touch
you heat me up with your whisper
you lure me in with your flaring eyes
we say goodbyes burning as the night dies

How are you?
I scream at the top of my lungs to the universe
So maybe you could hear it
In case you needed someone to ask you
To be able to open your bottled-up feelings
I know it's going to be okay
Maybe not now,
But I know it's soon

THE DREAM

The dream is to be given
A chance to escape reality
A chance to dream; to
Shoo away nightmares, that
Creeps, that lurks in the shadows.
To be able to fly high and free,
Soaring through the skies;
Untethered, free from the cage.

The dream is to wake up
Sane and wanting and breathing;
Still dreaming with wide opened
Eyes seeing the wonderful
Side of reality; away from
The monsters I've ran from.

You should have
Told me we were just friends
I would have never—

      Let you taste my lips
      Let you take me
      Let you imprison my heart

Just friends don't know
What each other's lips taste like

DRUNK DIALING MY THERAPIST

the phone starts ringing
in my ear, in my head
I hear her whisper

       "these drugs won't solve
       your problems for you,
       what you need is support,
       love, and community

to be touched
to be seen
to be validated
to be told you're enough
and you're doing all right

       and fine,
       these will help you
       balance some things
       but strength comes
       from the outside

it's not weak to ask for help."

the phone starts ringing
in my ear, in my head
I hear this at the end of the beep

       "please enter a valid phone number."

You've put me through notions
of not being able and capable
of loving you
when you said you're tired and done
all along
it wasn't really me,
tell me

AN OPEN LETTER TO SOMEONE
(because I don't have the guts to send this)

Can't tell if we're still in this together;
If we're gonna stay together longer.
I'm not sure you're ready to accept
These declarations to the universe:

I love you so much it physically hurts,
If we keep seeing each other, more
should be laid out on the table,
not just this, not just that, not those—

I deserve better. I deserve the best.
How can I keep you if you can't be that best?
Please don't keep leaving me on read.
I can't say hello when I'm on delivered.

I don't have the guts to tell you this
so I'm writing you a poem because
you told me to think of other ways
to tell you I miss you, I love you.

Honestly, I don't know. Do I care?
I don't know either, and I am
scared to find out next morning
you're no longer bleeding my name.

I know
you'd rather
give me pennies
than
give me
pieces of your heart

THAT'S PURE LOVE, THEY SAY

I spent a good amount of my years
digesting everything you've put
down my throat forcefully—
words, ideas, actions, thoughts

I spent a good amount growing up
spending these things on people
who didn't deserve them, how
their innocence flashed before my eyes

I can't tell whether who's lying.
But you can't keep talking
like you hate me and then
continue telling me you love me.

Love is not equated by the
amount of rice I have to kneel on,
how many sticks have to be broken,
or beating I have to take in.

But that's what true love is, they say.
They're just looking out for you.
The world is a cruel place and what's
better than being trained at your home

to take in all the incoming bullets
that life may fire at your direction.
I needed to grow, to learn, I'm confused—
to be better or worse? Fuck this.

Cinderella accidentally left her shoe and so the prince had a way to find her. I left pieces of my heart with you and as I walk my way home. I left pieces of my being and soul with every step I take so that you would find your way to me.

(but he never came)

MAYKENN LOVE
(Bantayan Island trip, April 2021)

Blooming flowers in Cloverfield green
I take a sip of this lime green drink
Shades of blue and unsettling winds
Unpacking bags, our love story begins

Touched my body, joints shaken
Warm skins touching, red lips
Making beds, tips touching end
My Maykenn love, your wayward heart

Conjoining, and then split
This is where the story ends
Slowly breaking, slowly falling apart
On the beach grass, last night spent

I thought we will forever be
Who we were on the first day

ghost of you

you remind me of your presence
with everything in my surrounding
apparitions of a love that once lived

I remember you in songs
I remember you in movies
I remember you in books

and I remember us,
every time each single one of those
come to an end

until we meet again

I'll see you tomorrow in the bench,
in the park we used to play in.
the lovely sunsets,
and your look when you're out of breath.
the dancing grass,
and all the noises we make and fuss.

I'll see you at 3pm,
the usual time and bring some lime.
And your silly old lame jokes about
why you got a buzz cut, and
how you are and will always be mine.

I'll see you when I see you,
not when you're with someone else, telling
your jokes and how you are theirs,
and they are yours.

Funny how I'm not funny,
Sitting at the same bench;
How my heart is wrenched.
Just sitting while the swings swing,
the grasses dance, the sun sets.

I'll see you when I see you;
I will try to never see you,
            until we meet again.

Did I make your
favorite music sound bad
or your favorite
movies feel horrible
or your favorite
book sound so cliché
or your favorite
food taste so bad

Or did I spoil
the taste of your love?

TO MY YOUNGER SELF

As you grow older and wander
take every feeling in
learn all those freaking lessons
let your heart learn pain
But never close it, don't go insane

you grew into things
you said you're
never going to be

(don't come near those guys, I know men)

PUBLIC SERVICE ANNOUNCEMENT

the players are here
the game is about to start
guard your heart
their plan is clear

He loved like he was just stacking pairs of shoes and slippers on a mat placed by the door. Forgot to arrange it back. Left with a mountain-full of pieces of lovers before.

(i'm one of it, i'm sure)

IF THESE WILD WINDS ARE YOURS
                    for The Brazen Youth,

you are a hurricane
shaking my being
leaving me on foot
your music soothes
your voice amazes
your song blazes
love screams wild
with you, I am beguiled

and though winds do not disturb
you are a hurricane
frenetic and wild
I am swept off my foot
leaving no room for hope

You gift me pain
Sealed with memories of a lifetime
When you left

And I gift you words,
You told me *no*

Caused by the pain you've caused me
You keep them forever bound in a book
I keep this too, in a box labeled *you*

'TIS THE REVOLUTION

Just know in time we will end him
Collectively, our love is our strength
History speaks loudly and clearly:
Love wins revolutions

'tis the massacre
'tis the abuse
'tis the foolishness
'tis what he's confused

These things will bring end
to an empire of men thinking
The world could be played by a few
of men, of goons, of monsters

To be locked up in dungeons.
'tis the season to be jolly.
Our love will scream loudly:
'tis the revolution that will end the misery.

How do i
let go of you
when you were
the definition
of *home*?

I love you,
I didn't mean to

I did love you
for the past
8 minutes or 8 months

Honestly,
I'm forgetting

I guess we're just
gonna live through this

When will we ever be a happy story?

Not once ever
Have I ever felt regret
Choosing you
Choosing this

Not once ever
Have I ever thought of
Letting go of you
Letting go of this

Clearly,
We aren't on the same page
You chose to end this
I chose to just walk away

Tell me
Why did we let go of the things
we really love most?

AN ARTIST ON DUTY

The steps weighed more
than the gaseous stars
that led me to you.

Every foot forward left pieces
of me I would never
be able to recover.

Trail tracks of mementos
and made-up memories
to craft this masterpiece.

An idea. A thought.
A collage of stardust
and broken dreams.

An art made of cracks
from shards and pieces
broken by our past.

Ben Elbert
November 1, 2021

for Ben,

you are a euphoric explosive blasting
through the walls of my one room
apartment, a caravan of all these mixed
feelings and meshed up signals,
scattering, wandering through all these
different directions. making me wonder,
wander, staring, breaking, kneading,
remolding myself back up to the way I was
before. i'm pointing north, towards the
opposite of where you're gonna be. I am a
peak. the tip of cold formation. you have
contorted me into this, to make me look
like something you'd accept. I no longer
am moving—i've risen. and i'm staying on
top of everything else you've told me i
won't become. I freed myself. no longer
am needing of your ecstatic thunderbolt.

Ben Hood
February 22, 2022

for Ben,

Jonson wrote me a letter in 1593
It says "free the wild, adventurous beast in you,
Explore the vast world that awaits you,
Let your freedom shake science,
Let 21 be that rising sun."

At 11,239 feet, I let my hands hurdle free
I hike mountains so up high
Letting my feelings go away in sigh
This may be Ben the second in the world
But you are first in mine

I go in worry-free, all for you is me
Every Man in His Humour would argue
Ben is not the end of it all
I am a wild, adventurous beast
Ready to take on the world, if it's you

Ben Heartbreak
April 14, 2022

for Ben,

How do we stay sane when we scream atop our lungs
Keeping your name off my lips. Red stains.
Your throwaway feelings you kept short. A red light.
How do I keep you off haunting my mind
Tracing your figure in the air. Red crayons.
Black paints and silver cloths. A red flag.
How do I start keeping you off my writings
Let you run free in the wild. No more red lines.
Broken promises and white lies. A stop light.
How do I push you away and make no one get hurt
I look up to your tower of sever. A peak.
Broken and madness and everything else. Bloody red.
Crimson kisses forever remembered. An end.

I am coming down now, following a red trail track.
When you said you liked her, what did you mean?
I still write your name and whole bunch other crap.
When you said I meant something, was I seen?

every once in a while
I would still crave
for the love you
once made me feel
for the world you
once built for me
for the paradise you
once showed me,

but never you.

MONDAYS ARE FOR HEARTBREAKS

And isn't it sad
to realize that we chose
to see past through the red lights
and ignore the waving red flags
because we were scared
we will never ever going
to feel *this* ever again?

Things that are needed to be done:

- Be happy and remove toxic people
- Move on and be happy with the things I do
- No regrets
- *Fall in love*
- Get broken and grow
- Never chase the same person again
- *Forget you*

THE LILIES IN YOUR BUROUGH

there are things I tell myself
secrets from vaults I only open at night
a case of emergency stories
to entertain myself with
or go-to laughing stock tales
in case I feel like crying myself to sleep
as if I'm truly scared of creating
a garden bed of lilies on my bed,
when things get out of hand
like when you get out of touch
how I became just a lily
alone fending for myself
on a bed you planted me in
in the middle of everything
wanting to finally cave in

I write you on these
blank pages as a
poem to let you know
that I still think of you

WE ARE ANALOGS

There are days I'm convinced
You've convinced me to think
I am the root cause of everything

There are days I'm convinced
That the way you tried
May be the root cause of everything

There are nights I think
That maybe we are just like
Everyone else, confused where
To begin, when to end this

And I guess, all that we really have left now is to move on
and accept things like the man we've always wanted ourselves
to be and be happy.

GOODBYE TO THE WONDERS

Playing Bridge card game;
Sat across me and your mom,
We write lovers under the coffee table.
Red wine breaths and stolen glances.
We laugh at jokes your dad makes;
Munching on cakes your mom baked.
Relaying messages through stares—
Hands held forever bound.
I kiss your cheeks goodbye
Wonder whether I'd see you tomorrow

I've always been afraid to say bye
Frightened of the uncertainties—
And wonders I may never get a hello.

I've always remembered,
You've always forgot.

this poetry
is my only memory
of you.

Love should not be the reason:

- Why you would stop growing
- Why you would forget the meaning of self-love
- Why you would forget that being happy with yourself is as beautiful as being happy with someone else
- Why the world would start moving to the other direction
- Why you would fall for people so much that you're willing to risk and break yourself
- Why you would despise it.

on days I feel empty
I fill myself with food
seemingly desperate
to fill this void.

your name
still leaves a
bittersweet taste
on my lips.

after years I realized
their efforts to silence my voice
meant
my voice held power
a revolution behind every echo
they're afraid of

a force that could
destroy systems
of tyrannies and regimes

Love is the air we breathe:
      the thin comforting air
      the beautiful blue sky
      so delicate it leaves us
      fascinated, baffled
      so left with questions
      we queue ourselves
      in line with pain
      that waters us—
      let us grow, and
      bloom beautifully.

How about a toast to me?

Maybe you could give this one up to me
Because finally, I'm free
For the record, I did fool myself
That I am doing this to hurt you
And make you realize how much I meant
I thought I was doing this to teach you a lesson
But now, I realize that this is more about me
Finally learning my lesson.

I will never break your heart

To be fair,
I was impressed
You've never given me any rose
But showered me with fields
Filled with variety of tulips.

I happen to remember
They symbolize chaste and
Unconditional love,
Maybe it isn't too late?

I love you in poems
that are yet to be written

I love you in words that are yet to be discovered.
I love you in sentences that are yet to be defined.

This is how we say good bye

Part 1
FADED

show me all the photos
we took together in summer
more sunny and light than bare.
Printed on polaroid papers
wanting to be seen
as ink becomes visible
love becomes unseen.
Aching to be felt
you faded along with your promises
more like despair than happiness rare.
It left me broken hearted
vulnerable and weak, easy to shoot.
I thought I caught the love
i've been telling the moon above
too proud to be taken aback
I live with this dream,
a dream of heartache and pain
caused by a love so vain.

Part 2
CUT-OFF

I still can feel the summer breeze
the warmth of your embrace
the feeling of your arms
draped around my naked body
how you kissed my temple
then to my neck and the back of my head
down towards where it ended.
I still can feel the heat
of a boiling tear wanting to escape
demanding it to be known
and the hurt to be felt.
I still can feel how it stung
when you'd kiss her goodbye
right in front of my naked eyes
how you'd embrace her in a hug
or how you'd text her even though
you are with me—or are you really?
I told you to stop.
And sometimes things have to be done
and this I tell you, my love
looking back to memories
is pretty and heartwarming
but you can't find home there

home is here,
home is present
and if you ever try to look,
in just a glimpse
i'd see my worth and
if you look back at me
i'd no longer be there,
now we will be the past
in the present that was
supposed to be the future,
now a lifetime.

Part 3
FACES OF BLACK

winter came and the cold winter breeze
embraced me,   you,   the both of us
as if it was concerned
that heat might cover
the both of us and
an even heater thing come
but it wasn't the air
I was so concerned of,
it was your actions,
honey, everyone who ever
called me *love* and *darling*
left me with unfulfilled promises
of a love that would last a lifetime
and swear
if you ever call me either
birds would fly high
waves of high current will build up
air of so strong winds would not just
blow houses and buildings
but this is winter
so it would just freeze
the time of me and you,
freeze the
distance

of

us

so *darling* tell me,
how did you guess the ending
when it's only the beginning?
Winter came and confusion ate me
I was torn between which was colder,
is it the weather or you?
Because I swear I could feel it
how these thousand islands
turned out to be just hundreds
how these rosemaries
were really poison ivy in disguise
how these books were really confessions
of love not fiction——I know
how your *I love you*s doesn't end
with that but rather with *just friends*:
I love you as a friend. But love,
just friends don't look at each other like that
nor knew how it feels to be touched,
to be sensed sensually. You wanted me,
but why not to the extent of keeping me?
Now *darling love*, tell me,
why did we stop?

I love you. I did not mean to.
I'm sorry. Winter left with you.

He is a masterpiece in the making
Made from pieces of himself
From trail tracks he left while leaving

and yes someday,
we would be brave enough
to let go of the things
that does not make us
happy anymore.

BRAVEHEART

I grapple with my heart on a plank sword
On bluebird days, still and unstirred
Shooting through the fields of green
Looking through the hundred different shades of blue
Stumped whether which side to lean on
Mad and demented to think clearly
I speak to my core in a loud voice

Great things are attained through
Doing everything and doing nothing
Great people know when to act and when not to
Special minds honed together with bravery
Are bestowed with valor and nobility
You are an extraordinary being shining
Never not be afraid to jump off the plank

Sometimes letting go is the best thing

Home is not where I come to be,
But it is with those I have come to be with.

I wake up every morning
covered with the night before—
your kisses, your touch
the rants you only told me,
the way your hand traces me,
your lips owning every inch of my skin.
I wake up every morning
with only the feelings you gave me,
without *you* to feel me.

I love my moon.
But I love more the sun you gave me.

But *your* sun that shine—
It keeps on setting.

I'M SO TIRED OF FLYING

I exist. This is what I am, this is
where I am meant to be.

I exist. I don't care if all the
universe conspire to take this all away
this is who I am,
this is what I need

I exist. All the troubles and keepsakes
have tried their best to strike me
yet I am still here
flying
soaring
and shining.

I exist. I breathe, I feel, I live.
I exist, and I know this is where
I needed to be.

All those longing days spent in dreaming,
In walking alone along the shore,
In wishing above every passing star,
In books I've read from your bedside table,
In music I've played from your collection.

All those missing nights spent in breathing,
In imagining you were here,
In hugging the pillow next to me
And breathing in the scent you left.

The days were counted with every rain,
The number of dandelions blown,
And the times I've spent wishing—
Of dreaming you've dreamt of me too.

UBREAKABLE

Yours words may chip some
parts of my body but it will
never break me.
I know who I am—
I am the architect who designed
such glorious structure;
I am the engineer that built this
piece, piece by piece;
I am the artist that made sure I'd
look good inside out;
I am the inspector that made sure
I'd be unbreakable,
fearless, unapologetic, flawless.
You see, I've come into terms with myself:
Those details you saw negative,
I've finally seen their value.
They are my greatest details,
Those things you see flaw:
They are my greatest assets.
They complete me, they make sure
I stay me, make sure I stay rare,
atypical, unconventional,
I stay weird, I stay freed.
You see, your words,
They no longer break me.
Those words I use patches, stacked one
By one with each thrown word, I've
made myself unbreakable.

all I ever wanna do is this
dance along with the waves
either on my drunk or sober state
under the twinkling night sky

i'd probably do it with you
skinny dipping in the dark
stripped from all the stress
of the world, for it to see

i'd probably do it tonight
dance with you and the waves
your hands cupping my bare ass
but I don't really care

all I ever wanna do is this
dance the night away
until the morning light shines
and we'd twinkle, glow golden.

OUT OF SORTS

Maybe it's the winds
Maybe it's the weather
Maybe it's the coffee this morning
Why am I even blaming everything else

Maybe it's the way you look
Maybe it's the way you feel
Maybe it's the way how I feel
Now that you no longer feel like home

Maybe I'm just tired
Maybe I'm confused
But one thing is for sure
I do feel like missing home

I still feel the warmth of your hand
Your finger tracing the indentations of my ribs
The soft touch of your skin against mine

I hear the sound of pleasure
Whenever our lips collide
And the electricity we feel
Flowing as if it connects us

I trace your figure in the fields
Your smile I see in these flowers
And the sparkles in your eyes,
I see them wherever I go

I miss how you eat my moans of ecstasy
How our bodies dance to the rhythm
How every inch of your skin
Fits perfect to mine—
As if you were made for me,
And I'm here for you to design.

I would never
turn the lights off
and will leave the door open
keep your tooth brush in the container
and leave your side of the bed empty
in case you finally decide
to come back

and he had been whispering over and over
 'come back, come back to me, come back
 come back to me, come back, come back to me'
and the echoes of silence and dystopia

I see your image in the distance
 'regrette rien'—'non, je ne regrette rien'
and the cries and wails of the none
all I could ever see is your face

and the fall of my hopes the he'd come back,
oh my love, he had been the most precious thing
one I could only imagine and hope for
I whisper the mourning of the one

I hear your voice in the distance
and even smell your scent from afar
I wrote you letters you never read
oh love, I took my heart and put it on the bed

I hear him say
       come back...
                come back to me...
come back...
         come back to me...

why do I crave sometimes
for your hug and comfort
even though those arms
gave me hurt and discomfort?

(*the familiar*)

NIGHT FRIGHTS

He was a world in my universe
It's all, everything I could offer
How it's daring for him to be all my fears
He gave me a sun to ease it over

But it was all temporary,
He was the sun, he gave me his sun
And it keeps on setting, over and over

Faith is the only thing I have

I thought
Faith would be my saving grace
from the hurt
from the abandonment

but it was my faith
in you
that led me to
the hurt
to the abandonment

THEATRE NERDS

Remember when we used to watch
Dear Evan Hansen and *Hamilton*
How you would smile at me when our song comes on
Remember how we'd dance and sing along

You'd grin to *For Forever*
How I'd lean my head to you
When *Only Us* comes along

Funny how I never told you
Requiem is my favorite song,
And I'd write countless requiems
And sing them for you

I still feel your arms
draped around my body
telling me *everything's gonna be okay*

VISIONS

I hear your name lingers along with the winds
fresh breeze, kisses and laces
running and running towards the ends
feeling your warmth near, seeing your traces

we finally come out to the light
risking our wayward hearts on the table
are we now really giving up this fight
all we have is to move on, *are we able?*

I hope I grow
Myself some love
Like how I grew
Some love for you

I wish my love for you
is the same as this pen I use
to write pieces of you I remember
so for each letter that I write
the ink of my love
decreases
decreases
decreases
until it runs dry

I took the risk
Just jumped into the open ocean
Not looking
At how dark it looked
How deep it looks
At the bottom
Not knowing
Its vast unknown

if love is just a mere dream
why does it wake me up
in the middle of the night
suddenly
like it was a 3D movie
in my mind
meant to scare me

I still wish
for the nights
when you own me
completely.

THE CHASE

Forever
we will be haunted
by the ghosts of our past
we left unanswered,
unresolved,
unforgiven

Forever
they will try to
tear us apart
ruin us
piece
by
piece

but only if
we let them

"make me the
happiest man
in the world"
he said

“can you
let me go?”

this is how we say goodbye

if I was not a love poet,
I would be something else completely
A stranger
I would feel like I was nothing
Like the dust on every
Left-behind things waiting
To be rediscovered,
Even though the chances
of people choosing me
are slim
I'd still bet
I'd still write
Even how shitty
I'd love
I'd write
I'd take the chances
Just to write you

USUAL

I couldn't bear doing the usual routines:
brushing my teeth, getting out of bed
cooking food for myself, or take a shower

yet I could talk to you for hours
or even write letters, exchanging emails,
pictures of what we're doing and plan to do

you're like a heroin i'm not supposed to take in,
yet I still do, and it's fast addicting

when the sun shines,
we step into the light;
willing and courageous.
let fear for the tomorrow
be felt and celebrated
but not let it drive.
let passion and love shower,
joy and empathy hover.

Let the day be its best,
Let no ray of darkness cloud,
Let no anger frustrate,
Let no shadow enshroud.

when the sun sets,
we love ourselves right.
we were ablaze and
we soared high for the day.
rest easy now and
be not afraid of what
the future might await.

SOME NIGHTS

there are nights I crave you
or how we stay up late doing things
going to parks, or having night walks,
pulling all-nighters to watch our favorites,
I write while you read all my poems

there are nights I sink
missing the feeling of warm touch, warm hugs
how your lips would cover mine
how I savour the feelings you pour
how your part of the bed would sink
or how I wake up to you cooking

there are nights I realize
it's not you I've been missing
maybe at least not who you are now
but who you've been

When dawn comes, we tell ourselves:
good job, thank you, I love you.
Words we needed to hear to
keep us intact, to stop our bleeding.

When dawn comes, we let our hearts rest,
let ourselves be free from the sadness,
from all the things that break us.
It's okay to be tough and it's okay to be human.

If only we can always cry ourselves to sleep.
If only we can shut our hearts down.

THE WITCH

'don't go near her' they say
'she'd rip your heart out'
and all those nasty things about me
or at least a version they crafted
a character they think I've mastered

I've got standards, high as skyscrapers
I don't break hearts; the hearts break on their own
I patch up my clone, they do it on their own.

THE WITCH (part 2)

you still took a step closer
despite all the warnings
a daredevil, a foolish player
it's danger, you keep bringing

you took my hand
and my wayward my heart followed suit,
you brought me the moon
and declared me your world

you shut out all the bricks
and stones that they threw at us
all the noise and quiet
you brought me peace and
certainty in the uncertain
taught me love and
sorcery and lust

you threw me off your back
like a dust, like a metal with rust
inculpated me like I was not
who you were dreaming of
wrote me as a nightmare
instead of a daydream come to life

you taught me how to dance with fire
like a prep, a training, the beginning
of an awful ending you said
we'd both write together till the end, on
the edge of the world

you were the first one to throw the fork
and you lit up the stake for your sake
for centuries we were taught
to fear the witches—powerful women
they can't control and handle

when it should be men
the ones who haunt and killed them
we should be fearing

I watched your back as you walk away
Left me with all those promises you made me keep
I put them in my treasure chest with an X
I guard it with all my defiant heart
I keep it as more than just a memento
A reason for you to come back my way
I write you poems and stories with my blood
A bath tub full of my tears I cried for you
I draw your eyes for me to stare at
I still paint your broad shoulders over and over
Something I've kept, something I've remembered
It's printed in my mind to be kept forever
I keep the lights on, keep the door open
I get on my knees every night before I go to sleep
I offer my heart for you, I devote my whole soul
I sleep with stinging in my eyes and
Wake up with a dream of hope you'd regret it all

Oh the little things I'd do to lose you again

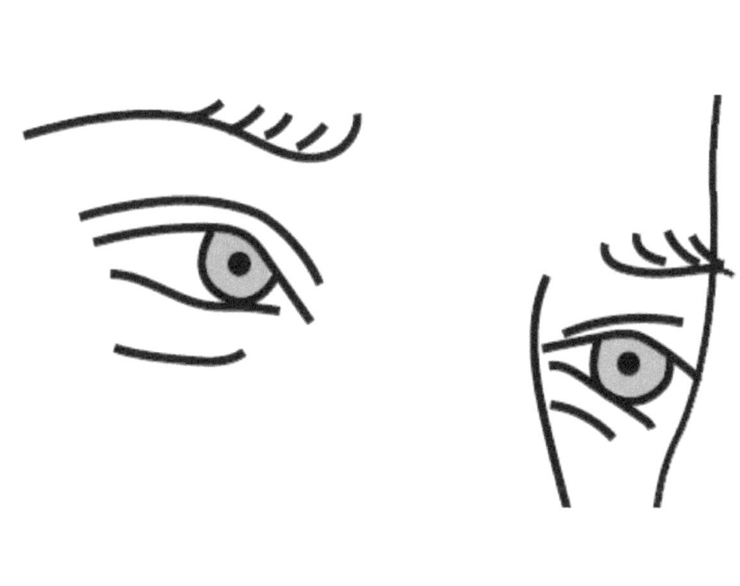

Loving you is being selfishly selfless.

tell me where did i
actually go wrong—

was it that i rushed you
or that i built you—

projected and made
this image of what you

should be, when you aren't
and it's sad truly

heartbreaking.

IN THE SHADOWS

Are we really scared
of the dark? Or the

things that happen
in it and the monsters

that lurk. Are we scared
of who we might become

and what we might do
when we're left thinking

we're scared. When we're
vulnerable. Ready to be

preyed on by the insecurities
we let define ourselves.

Is it really darkness or
is it really, truly us?

I love you with all my aching heart.

HE MUST END

He—a masterpiece of great significance
Crafter of nothingness and everything
A magnificent illustration of all things beautiful
Illusion conjugating treachery with divergent colors

In stillness we achieve great things—
We have always since time immemorial
Imagined in so many lifeforms
Achieved through so many different ways

Yet he keeps trying to search for something
For all we know it might be nothing
There may be nothing beyond or beneath us
He still does, he keeps going on

Why go on?
Why keep trying?

And then, there was me in between everything
He says I *was* magnificent, spectacular
A cluster of stars, of all things bright and beautiful
A galaxy of true beauty that can only ever be discovered

But he says
Beneath all my sublime surfaces he found nothing
No lofty details and bits and bobs
He must not be declared, he whispers

Why not keep me?
Why not let me go?

In united movement we found our common ground
Only then we discover this *something* is so foreign
We try to reach for different ways
We try to expand in so many routes

And so he does the next best thing
Resorted to a plan that will keep him afloat
Option that will push me astray
Our boat no longer in uniformed adrift

And so I say
Above all the things he finds insignificant
There is beauty worthy to be in scriptures
I declare, *he must end*

Also by Vhon Michael

Every Moment Was You
Midnight Memories

ABOUT THE AUTHOR

VHON MICHAEL is an 18-year old writer and activist currently based in Cebu. He loves to write, dance, watch movies and series, take photos of random things, and eat. He works with several international organizations to address climate change, gender inequality, lack of mental health awareness, and inaccessibility of education, and has been featured in many international news and media. He is currently a university student studying political science, international relations and economics. He is also obsessed with Taylor Swift!

With love and gratitude to;

Xaniel, who has encouraged me to write a book and has inspired most of the poems on this one.

Llorenç, who has inspired a lot of the poems that I wrote during my trip to Bantayan Island that made it into this book.

Sheena, Katrina, Azalhea, Jennelyn, Joshua and Dexter, my best friends. Who have had my back since day one. Thanks for recording the stupid shits I do when I get drunk.

Iris, my virtual bestie whom I share a lot of my secret crushes with. Mitzi, Tara, Aishwarya, Jett, Rodrigo, Ava, Evie, Jahnavee, Lili, Sophie, Brooke, Tessie, Phoebe, Ayshka, Ben, and my entire FFFD family, for all the love and support.

Taylor Swift, The Brazen Youth, The Greeting Committee, Honeywater, Phoebe Bridgers, Lorde, The Paper Kites, Axel Flovent, Nate Poshkus, and many more, thank you for your music.

To my followers, you have been supporting me all throughout. My readers, you never failed to amaze me with all of your love and support for me and my works. Thank you and I love you.

vhonmichael.com
linktr.ee/vhonmichael

FACEBOOK   Author Vhon Michael Tobes
INSTAGRAM   @vhonmichaell
TWITTER   @vhonmichael
LINKEDIN   Vhon Michael Tobes
MEDIUM   @vmtobeswrites

For collaborations, reviews, imprint for review email
vhonmichaelbooks@gmail.com

www.ingramcontent.com/pod-product-compliance
Lightning Source LLC
La Vergne TN
LVHW041518170726
843492LV00005B/1568